A

MISCELLANY

Poems, Anecdotes, Articles, Fiction, Biography & Mum's Poems

By Sylvia Sharples

<u>Dedication</u>

To my mother Marie Williams
(1916-1997)

I hope she would have been proud
of my efforts – she taught me well!

Thanks to Mike Scantlebury and Jane
Wood and all members of the Creative
Writing Group from Gail's Kitchen, who
nurtured my latent writing skills.

I N D E X

Poems   Page   1

Anecdotes   Page   45

Articles   Page   111

Fiction   Page   130

Biography   Page   156

Mum's Poems   Page   173

ALLOTMENT SAGA

A plot of land to grow our own
A place where seedlings could be sown
Obstacles would be overcome
Hopes and dreams for rain and sun.
Committees formed and rules compiled
Little did we know how much a trial
It would be of dogged determination
and guile

Just to get a piece of green amidst
tarmac and houses
So we could put flowers in our vases.
We hoped to grow our own potatoes,
Cabbages, sprouts and red tomatoes
Instead of in tubs on paths and patios

. The Council again could not deliver
Negotiations went on forever
Resulting in no commitment or
endeavour

With us getting to the end of our
tether.

We still have dreams of our bit of land
Where we could gather with our hand
The tender shoots from our green
fingers
And listen to natures finest singers

One day we will – if the gods are kind,
Stand on our patch of ground,
And tend our plants all around,
And wonder at all the fuss
Caused by red tape, which we did
curse,
Because all we wanted was to GROW
OUR OWN!

March 2010

ODE TO CREATIVE WRITING

A farewell to all who passed this way
Who put pen to paper every Tuesday
Songs were sung and poems read,
Much better than lying home in bed.

Hidden talents were uncovered
Sad memories of past lovers,
Happy times, missing cats and lost
causes
Were put on paper in many clauses.

Mike and Jane were a guiding light
To those who were afraid to write
Their thoughts in verse and song
So they really helped us all along.

We hope to meet again another time
And continue with our song and rhyme.
Maybe some will do other things

It's still amazing what community brings.
Adieu!

April 2010

NEW HOME

Circumstances again dictate
The need to once again relocate.
Feelings of fear and trepidation
About the City's reputation.

Boxes packed, keys collected
House is ready for inspection.
Seems OK, wonder how it'll be?
Curious neighbours come to see.

Didn't expect to be accepted
A few smiles were detected.
Someone offers us a cup of tea
Our mood turns to one of glee.

Think we'll get along quite fine
We thought we'd be maligned.
In fact I think we'll stay,
And never live to rue the day!

PROGRESS

Another building hits the dust
Do you really think they must?
Trees uprooted, chopped in bits
Homeless blackbirds and bluetits.

Rubbish strewn along the street
Empty cans alone to greet
The new arrivals heart did sink
Why big business didn't think.

Cranes move in to clear the sites
Do the locals have no rights?
Memories and identity do matter
All that's left is noise and clatter.

Big business draws up schemes
Which on the drawing board seems
To offer an outsider's vision
Often acclaimed on television.

Promises made to consult and get
approval
Decisions made behind closed doors.
Councils say it will be better
Then you end up with the letter.

Time to gather all the neighbours
To see if they can find some saviours
Who can champion their cause
To overturn the legal clause

Progress is what it's called
New buildings are then installed.
High rise blocks in the sky
Which gravity does defy.

What happened to the consultation
With architects, councils, and their
exultation
They'd adhered to their remit
But all they wanted was the permit.

The planners have again won through
Lip service given to all of you
They get their way again
It will never ever be the same!

CHRISTMAS FAYRE

Memories of the simple things
With puppets dancing on their strings
Stockings hanging on the bedpost
Hoping for things we wanted most.

Parents looked on with pride
As offsprings' eyes opened wide
When they found what was inside
Games were played wrappings cast
aside.

Food aplenty on the table
Hardly a thought about the stable
The meaning of the feast was lost
All that mattered was the cost.

Time is now to turn the clock
And once again take stock
Of why the feast is provided
To celebrate and not be divided.

Rejoice and shout to friend and foe
We want good seeds to scatter and sow
Do not be afraid to tell the world,
Undo your banners that have been
furled.

September 2010

NEXT DOOR

Next door they are mowing the grass –
Not good for hay fever.

Next door there is hardly a sound –
We wonder if someone's still around?

November 2010.

<u>AUTUMN</u>

Autumn leaves are falling fast
The Sun long shadows cast
The clocks have now gone back
Nature's course is well on track.

Time to sort the garden out
Before old Jack Frost's about
Put the gardening tools away
Make ready for another day.

The birds have flown to a warmer climb
But will return when Spring is nigh
The slugs have gone to ground
Not even a small one can be found.

Pavements are strewn with gold
Which November winds unfold.
Were they really bright Green
When in April they were first seen?

Time for cosy evenings by the fire
Play the flute or learn the lyre.
Maybe even drink mulled wine
We know everything will be just fine.

November 2010

TECHNOLOGY

It's hard to think of times past
When the world was not so vast
News took weeks to filter down
To every village and every town.

Today world events are broadcast
In a flash on TV's, radios and podcast.
No time to digest the facts
And decide how we should react.

Everyone is in the public eye
CCTV makes it hard to deny
Where we are throughout the day
Whether we are at work or play.

Big brother is watching you -
We never thought that would come
true!
Too late now for protestations
We have to live with our indignations.

We did not read our crystal ball
Warnings were written on the wall.
Feeble voices whispered their dismay
But technology is here to stay.

November 2010

EMILY

She's full of fun and daring do
Quick of wit and clever to
She has grown up fast
Childhood has soon past.

Her unicycle she mastered well
The envy of many we hear tell.
Circus people asked for lessons
And perhaps some learning sessions.

Stilt walking was next in line
This too she managed fine.
Now you see her walking tall
With only the occasional fall.

A lovely person whom we adore
With her around we'll never be poor.
Another teenage birthday's here
She fills our life with happy cheer.

In life she should go far
Soon she'll be driving a car.
Time flies by you'll agree
But family she'll always be.

Nanna Syl
29th December 2010

NEW YEAR THOUGHTS

I wonder what this year will bring?
Maybe more verse and songs to sing?
Perhaps more stories will abound
With which our fertile minds resound.

Our pens are poised and at the ready
With many words coming fast and
steady.
Will another book be written?
The writing bug has really bitten.

With our mentors Mike and Jane
Our modesty was long since slain.
We wait with anticipation for the next
session
Who says we're in the middle of
recession?

With inhibitions banished out the door
It will be time again to take the floor.

The tape recorder is once again in place
Recording words for Salford Radio's
space.

David Cameron's drastic economic
measures
Should in no way curtail our pleasures.
We should continue writing on our own
After all pens and paper don't need a
loan.

So keep on writing as in the past
Our words and verses will certainly last.
Our memories cannot be taken away
We'll be inspired to write again another
day.

January 2011

THE BBC IS COMING

The BBC has a new address
Down at Media City no less!
They have spent loads of dosh
So it will all look posh!

Salford has always been ahead of her
time
Whether it be paintings, song or rhyme
The image of grime has long been
outgrown.
Our City now wears her latest gown.

Proud as ever to welcome new friends
Embracing these new fangled trends
Dockers no longer toil and work with
ships
Pleasure craft now take the trips.

The Street is due to move there soon
The end of an era but still the same
tune.
We wonder what Ena and Martha
would think
Now that they're moving the kitchen
sink?

Where once docker's feet trod the
ground
And ships came homeward bound
Media moguls now take their place
And life has a different pace.

The giant cranes lay idle now
And winds of change begin to blow
Breathing new life into Salford Quays
Bringing prosperity which is sure to
please.

The skilled people from the North
Will easily prove what they're worth.
Success is theirs for the taking
No going back or forsaking.

We hope it all works out well
Only time alone will tell
Who knows what tomorrow will bring?
Except the birth of a new Spring.

A VALENTINE

You wash the dishes
And give me many kisses.
You're always there
Often sitting in your chair.

We walk along life's path
Sometime we have a laugh.
It's not all plain sailing
When health seems to be failing.

You bounce back like a ball
When I think you are about to fall.
For 14 years we've managed life's ups
and downs
With I think not too many moans.

I suppose we were meant to be
I'm sure that you will agree.
We have adapted to each other's ways
Hopefully to the end of our days.

IN BLOOM

Winter time is nearly done
Time for us to have some fun.
The sun is at last getting stronger
We won't have to wait much longer.

Get hanging baskets out of storage
Replenish with some new foliage
Time again to start to grow
For our In Bloom annual show.

Neighbours peeping over fences
Looking through our poor defences
Competition is a healthy thing
Who knows what that will bring.

Nature will soon be in full flower
The plants will need their daily shower.
Hosepipe bans we can do without
"Not again!" We often shout.

Time now to sit back and gaze
At myriad colours all ablaze
Fuchsia, honeysuckle and the poppy
Many artists have tried to copy.

The In Bloom judges will soon appear
And everyone will give a cheer.
We aim to get a higher grade
From all our work that's on parade.

March 2011

NATURE'S REVENGE

Oil And gas and nuclear power
Are we living in an ivory tower?
Nature seems to show who's boss
Then we begin to count the cost.

It's time for us to now take stock
Or all our heads will be on the block
All of nature lives in peace
Man alone takes the golden fleece.

We should consider what is right
It's time now to see the light.
We should not pander to our greed
Only take that which we need.

Poverty and need is all around
Crops are dying in barren ground.
Climate change is moving fast
For many peoples the dye is cast.

Resolutions should be made
For new foundations to be laid.
To consider each and every nation
And help them out of deprivation.

March 2011

NATURE'S ENERGY

The long winter days are past.
The sun longer shadows cast.
The clocks went back some days ago
Time for plants to thrive and grow.

Trees have woken from their sleep
Slowly green leaves begin to creep.
The miracle of spring is all around
Bringing life to barren ground.

Earth's cycles are slowly changing
Due to man's selfish re-arranging.
When will the wake-up call arrive
To enable the world to survive.

Earth's bounty taken at an alarming
rate
To feed the lorries carrying freight.
What right have we to plunder?
One day it will all be put asunder.

Just because we think we're right
To extract the oil by day and night.
Time now to stand back and think
Before the world goes over the brink.

April 2011

SCULPTURES

Sculptures all tell their unique stories
About countless deities and their
glories.
Man has used his many gifts of art
To symbolise and then impart
A glimpse of a world now past
Not realising they would ever last.

Churches, mosques, palaces and places
Are all adorned with many faces.
Cultures have been immortalised in clay
With other materials which survive
today.
We'll never really know the truth
Unless we can find some proof.

Today Time Lines are in vogue
Words are written without a brogue
Technology means our past isn't lost
Records can be kept at little cost

Future generations can easily see
What their ancestors used to be.

We all have our part to play
Writing with pen or sculpting clay.
Everyone should leave a legacy
Not to do so would be a tragedy.
Our children's children will then know
How we flourished in times long ago.

May 2011

NATURE

Green turns to gold and brown of every
hue.

Leaves fall and squelch under boot and
shoe.

Autumn creeps upon us before winter's
icy blast.

But nature's spring awakening cannot
be outclassed.

September 2011

SUMMER

The summer came and went so fast
Even though we knew it wouldn't last.
The sense of loss is felt all round
It crept away without a sound.

TREASURE

Parks and gardens are our treasures
Once the haunt of the privileged few
Now we can use them for our pleasures
Because the gentry couldn't pay their
dues

We should now take up our rights
Cherish and conserve without reserve.
No longer can we bemoan our plight.

<u>PARKS</u>

Parks are here to stay
Some are hidden away
Some you pass on the way
Try to visit one each Sunday.

September 2011

XMAS CARD (Roy)

Time passes quickly every day
I wish you happiness today
And throughout the coming year
Cherish those you hold most dear.

Time never ever stands still
So enjoy each moment as you will.
Blessings should be counted
Of hardships you've surmounted.

Be proud of who and what you are
Give thanks to your guiding star.
Someone's looking after you
Who is constant and will be ever true.

Sylvia xxx
(2011)

A LAMENT

It should be safe to walk round here
Without being worried and full of fear.
What right had he to pull the trigger
Is a question that his hard to figure.

A young man killed in his prime
Well before his allotted time.
His family stricken with sadness and
grief
For a son stolen from them by this
thief.

We need to put an end to this slaughter
It could have been your son or
daughter.
The community has suffered severe
shock
We're sorry we cannot turn back the
clock.

There must be an answer out there
Why someone caused this sad affair.
We should all be vigilant and aware
That someone round here really
doesn't care.

A vigil was held with great respect and
sorrow
For a stranger who will never see
tomorrow.
There was little else we could do more
Than to show we'd been shocked to the
core.

R.I.P Anuj Bidve

January 2012

OLYMPICS

From Mount Olympus to our island
nation
The sacred flame has reached its
destination.
It's time for us to line up for the start
In which everyone can now take part.

The stage is set with records to beat
As we watch all the world's elite
Compete as they did in ancient times
Long long ago in sunnier climbs.

(alternative)
Cheering on the world's athletic elite
As they now have chance to compete
For medals of bronze, silver and of gold
As each event on its merit will unfold.

January 2012

SECRET GARDEN

Across the field and down the lane
The old man went tapping his cane.
From a childhood long since past
Memories came flooding in so fast.
Would the house remember him
Or was its memory also dim?

As the gate came slowly into sight
The house looked in a terrible plight.
His step quickened as he reached the
wall.
He had to be careful he didn't fall.
Would the garden still be there
Like it was when his hair was fair?

Through tangled weeds and a bramble
bush
He huffed and puffed and gave a push.
What a sight greeted his eyes.
His feelings he couldn't disguise.

Tears of joy fell down his cheek
And he lovingly took a quick peak.

Someone with tenderness care and love
Had planted some flowers including
foxglove.
Perfume and masses of colour were all
around
Birdsong and busy bees was the only
sound.
Everything in nature was in its full glory.
Telling of the secret garden in this
story.

May 2012

MY SECRET GARDEN

My secret garden is a very special place.
From outside the house there's not a
trace
Of what lies behind the red back gate.
Mother Nature's creations are truly
great.

There's hebes, hydrangeas and flowers
aplenty
And a tree guarding them like a sentry.
Spring was very cold but time's moving
on
And we really do need some summer
sun.

Bees and butterflies will soon come
along
And maybe birds will sing their
evensong.
Time to sit quietly and drink in the glory
Of my special secret garden in this
story.

May 2012

<u>PERSEVERANCE</u>

Years of meetings and confrontation
Has at last turned into great elation.
"A lost cause!" the sceptics scream,
"You'll never realise your dream".

Money and land have now been found
So we can dig and till the ground.
A new venture for our community
Which we must grasp with impunity.

A lot more hard work is still needed
Before our allotments can be seeded.
Time now to plan our future
In the realms of agriculture.

A sense of well-being and good health
With home produce adding to our
wealth.
Dormant genes stirring deep inside

"What shall we grow?" We must now decide!

We'll provide for those less able
With a harvest for their table.
Full of pride that we did succeed
In a battle against giants – indeed!

July 2012

ANECDOTES

DAY TRIP TO IRELAND

It was a day In January in the late 60's and my then partner had purchased a converted trawler from a guy in White Rock, Northern Ireland.

We had waited days for a suitable forecast to go and collect the boat, there had been nothing but gales. Now the weather was set fair so we booked the midnight ferry, hurriedly collected our gear together. The gear consisted of pots, pans, sleeping bags life jackets, flares and enough food to last at least 3 days. We looked like hillbillies with our noisy rucksacks jingling along.

A friend of ours Johnny had a skipper's ticket and was a Manchester Ship Canal pilot and had offered to bring the boat over to a boatyard in Tarleton, where the boat was going to be refurbished.

We arrived in Belfast about 6am, gathered our belongings and went to get a taxi to White Rock. There were dozens of people queuing at the taxi ranks, armed soldiers were patrolling the docks, quite a culture shock. The whole area was very tense. Taxi drivers were walking up and down the lines of people asked where they were bound for. Lots were refused a taxi but we were lucky, White Rock seemed to be ok.

We bundled our gear into the cab and explained why we had such strange luggage.

We arrived at the house in White Rock, which belonged to the owner of the boat, who it turned out was a member of the judiciary. We were ushered into a small visitors' room. We had left our gear on the doorstep.

Suddenly, very quietly, a housekeeper appeared and her employer asked her to bring us tea and toast. She hardly spoke a word. A large tray was brought in with the tea a toast. We were really hungry.

We soon demolished all the toast and marmalade and sat back. Next another lot of toast and marmalade appeared as if by magic. Johnny and I had the same sense of humour –no words were spoken and I daren't look at him or I would have given way to hysterics, so we nodded and ate the second lot. We thought that was it, but no – yet another lot of toast appeared, this happened several times. It's a wonder we didn't choke ourselves.

Now it was down to business, the boat the Golden Dawn, had been brought off her mooring in Strangford Lock and was alongside the small pier. We were given a tour of the boat, paperwork completed and everything checked for our impending voyage. The owner told us there was some peat for the pot belly stove in the fo'c'sle. He had arranged for a pilot to take us through the loch where local knowledge was essential.

We reached the end of the loch and said farewell to our pilot it was now up to us to cross the Irish Sea heading for the River Ribble. It would take many hours.

It was freezing cold so we decided to light the fire – none of us had used peat before. It must have been too damp as the whole of the boat filled with acrid smoke. So the fire was out of the question. We had to heave to until we could see where we were going.

We took it in turns to steer, my partner and I under Johnny's directions as he needed to sleep before taking the night watch when we would be passing the Isle of Man.I found it difficult to sleep so was awake for most of the voyage. The sea was flat clam, we were so lucky to be underway.
Around 10 o'clock that night I was in the wheelhouse keeping Johnny company, when we were passing close

to the Chicken Rock off the Isle of Man. We had managed to get some music on a small transistor radio, when suddenly blasting loud and clear came the theme from The Onedin Line which was popular at that time. We couldn't stop laughing, it was a magical moment. The rest of the voyage passed without mishap and at dawn we were approaching Morecambe Bay, when a thick sea mist set in. We heard ships passing some distance away, the entrance to the Ribble would be difficult to find under these conditions so the skipper said it was better to come to an anchor and hope the mist would clear during the morning.

We organised an anchor watch and two went below to grab an hour's sleep. We were on a time schedule to make the boatyard at Tarleton at high water as that was the only time we could get through the lock when the canal and river were the same height. We were quite concerned as it would mean spending another 24 hours at sea if we couldn't make the high water deadline.

A few hours later the mist had cleared so we upped anchor and set off for the River Ribble, we then had to find the smaller River Douglas which led to the canal at Tarleton. This river was difficult to navigate, just little sticks, marking the channel. We just made it in time and the water had levelled in the loch and we sailed into Tarleton.

It was a memorable trip and I still laugh when I see marmalade and toast and hear The Onedin Line theme tune.

Happy days!

A TYPICAL DAY ABOARD A TRAWLER

All the fishing gear checked the day before, engine oil, and fuel checked, store cupboard, water container filled. Now we had to wait for the tide to come into the dock so we could get underway.

Warm clothes essential, it's always cold at that time of the morning. The tide arrives, we didn't need a clock, as soon as the water reached the fourth stone on the wall we had enough water to cast off the ropes.

The trip to the fishing grounds would take about 2 hours. One hour from port to Puffin Island off the Coast of

Anglesey, distance about 6 miles, against the incoming tide. It would take another hour to reach the fishing grounds.

The skipper would now be thinking of where best to shoot the gear, me the deck hand would stow all things in the fo'c'sle, the galley and on deck ready for action. It was now time to go down to the galley to make tea and toast for breakfast, not knowing when we would next eat. It depended on how much fish was in the first haul.

At this hour of the morning, if it was summer, we often saw a pod of dolphins making their way down the bay, coming out of the water two at a time really enjoying themselves. It was a wonderful sight.

At the fishing grounds the net was shot and the first tow started. The next two hours seemed to drag waiting to see if the skipper had chosen the right place to fish. During this time, the engine was checked and the bilges for any leaks, you never know with a wooden boat. The engine room is only about 3ft 6in high and smells of oil and diesel and is very hot.

Time up and ready to haul, oilskins donned, winch started and slowly the gear came up, once the net was up to the blocks on the stern the boat was turned in a circle so the cod end (the money end) was alongside amidships. Ropes were pulled tight to keep the fish in and the lifting strop fixed to the jilson to heave the bag aboard. It was suspended just above the deck so the cod string could be opened to let the fish onto the deck.

At this point there were gulls everywhere, on the gunnels, on the radio aerials between the masts and the noise was deafening. Any small fish which went over the side were soon gobbled up. The skipper kicked through the fish to see if it was worth shooting again on the same patch or we may have to steam a bit further out. The cod end was tied and blessed (a quick spit) and the boat straightened ready to shoot again.

Once the gear was in the water, the task of grading and sorting the different types of fish ready to be gutted began, minimum sizes checked. You were only allowed two undersize fish in a 5 stone box (about 400 small plaice) and if the fishery patrol came aboard it could be a £2000 fine. European rules, had introduced log books. This had to be filled in after each haul, you had to guess the live weight, the gutted weight and finally how many discards. This was quite a tall order for a two-handed crew. It was unbelievable the amount of rubbish in the form of plastic cups, cans, empty bottles, small stones, starfish, etc. came out of the cod end. Not exactly the image of Captain Bird's Eye!

Speed was now essential to gut the fish, get it down below out of the sun and wind, or it would not be marketable. Ice it up stacking the boxes so they wouldn't roll or move around with the motion of the boat. "No rest for the wicked!" as the saying goes, it would be time to get the deck ready for the next haul, which wouldn't be long. Not much time for a cuppa!!

I used to gut into a bucket and when all the fish was attended to, used to throw it behind the boat and the gannets came from near and far diving down for the titbits. It was a wonderful sight they are magnificent birds.

We mostly had two or three tows then it was time to get the gear aboard and stowed ready to return to port. Usually a 2hr trip, during which time the last haul was sorted and put down below into the fish hold. Decks had to be washed with the deck hose ready to land the fish. If we were in time to catch the fish house open, we would land on return to port, if not, we had to land on the tide the next day. If the tide was too early the next day we would go and have a couple of tows and then land the two lots together on the afternoon tide.

At the end of the first day, the net had to be strung up so we could clear all the weed and rubbish out of the net ready for the next day. We had to check there were no holes in the net, if there were these would have to be mended. If the damage was too great we had to bend another net on and mend the other when we weren't out fishing.

This day would be about 14 or 16 hours long before we could get to the fo'c'sle to wash and make a meal, inevitably our own fish, nothing ever tasted so good. We would then talk over the day's events, have a couple of glasses of cider, wait for the shipping forecast around midnight, so to bunk and up again for an early start weather permitting. Then the process would start all over again.

A couple of days later we would find out what our fish had made at market. Some would be bought locally by the chefs from the big hotels on Anglesey, the rest would be transported by the merchant to Grimsby for the open market. If we had skate wings these would be sent by train to Billingsgate for auction.

No matter what fish we caught, we only ever seemed to average £10 for a five stone box of fish across all varieties after taking out expenses, including ice, fuel, landing charges both ends and berthing fees.

Trawling is a way of life, the elation of being at sea, hunting an unseen quarry, the highs and the lows, nature in the raw etc. more than made up for the money side, as long as we had enough to survive through the Winter when we did not go fishing.

Sylvia Sharples (ex fisherwoman)
May 2010

PORT PENRHYN, NORTH WALES - WINTER 1975

In the summer of 1975 I ran away to sea to serve as crew on a commercial trawler. I was a learner "deckie", being shown how to gut fish and a whole world of marine jargon. I had always wanted to go to sea and now it had become a reality. My personal life was in tatters and I needed space and time to sort myself out.

I was 32yrs old and a woman – superstition stated a woman on a boat was trouble and bad lucky. This did not deter the skipper who liked a challenge. He ignored all the comments and set about teaching me "the ropes".

I had left all my possessions where I had lived and arrived with a suit of oilskins, my sea boots and a pressure cooker. The only things I thought may be of some use on a boat.

I learned net mending, all about engines, pumping the bilges, scrubbing the boat's hull and all manner of different aspects of life afloat. Commitment had to be absolute to make it work. I had no shore base so this was now my home and work place.

We went fishing whenever tides and wind allowed. Money was always tight as fish markets go up and down but we still had other financial commitments. The boat had a small mortgage which was almost paid up with Lombard North Central a commercial bank. The work was hard and very physical but very rewarding mentally. A way of life I had dreamed of.

One day in September as we were coming back to port after a day's fishing, the engine sputtered and made a big bang and then complete silence. We were adrift in the middle of Puffin Sound with a flood tide and were between rocks and a lighthouse on one side and Puffin Island full of rocks on the other. We were in danger of being wrecked.

The skipper, an ex-lifeboat mechanic, ran for'ard and literally threw the large anchor over the bows and managed to kedge (steer) the boat between the rocks. When the anchor just touched the bottom, the boat went round in a circle, and so we pirouetted to safer waters where we finally dropped anchor.

The Menai Straits is full of shipping hazards and we now had to get help and be towed to port if there was anyone listening on the radio. It was a Saturday and there were not many other large vessels working. Our boat weighed 30 tons dead weight so we needed a boat with power enough to take us in tow.

After several calls on the VHF radio, we faintly heard a reply. Our ship's batteries were running down as we had no power from the main engine. We managed to get the message across that we were stranded in The Straits. The skipper of this private yacht radioed that he would be with us in about an hour as there wasn't enough water for him to get out of the dock at that moment.

We kept an anchor watch and waited for what seemed an eternity. Time was running out for us to get into port as the tide would soon be turning. The other boat came alongside and once we had a tow rope aboard we had to haul the anchor by hand, a difficult task as the boat weighed 30tons dead weight, and of course we had no power to the winch as we were broken down.

It's every skipper's dread to come back to port on the end of a tow rope, and usually meant it could be very costly for repairs. In the past we had been the tow boat so this was reverse roles.

Once we were safely moored we took stock of the situation and it was soon evident that the old engine had literally died. Our options were few, we had to get mobile as soon as possible as without an engine we would get no wages, and there were still a couple of months of the year left before the winter weather arrived.

We went to our bunks with heavy hearts. We hadn't landed our fish it was still iced up down the fish hold but would have to wait until Monday before we could off load it. In the meantime we had to make plans for replacing the engine.

Monday came and we had to haul the fish up a 12ft wall onto the quay by hand. By this time tongues were wagging round the quay saying it was proof a woman aboard a trawler was trouble and we would never set sail again. We ignored the comments and set about finding another engine. We searched the appropriate papers and found a place in Wrexham which dealt in ex-admiralty engines. A phone call later we were on our way to see if it was suitable. We had some rough measurements but also had to find someone to take the old engine away once we had lifted it onto the quay.

We were working on a shoe string budget, and we managed to do a deal for another engine with ours being taken in part exchange. We arranged delivery and had about a week to get the old engine out of the engine room and onto the quay. Getting a 2 ton engine out of the engine room and into the fish hold for a straight lift onto the quay was a mammoth task.

The dock had been built in the 1800's and next to our berth was a fixed hand operated crane which we planned to use for the task. We couldn't afford to hire a crane. We set to work and with the help of blocks and tackles we slowly inched the engine up a 9in step from the engine room and into the fish hold. We got the handle for the crane and it took two of us to turn it and slowly the engine was brought ashore.

Our engine arrived and we had to winch that aboard onto the deck and put the other one onto the wagon. We were shattered but at least we had another engine. Without being too technical we found to our dismay that the gearbox wouldn't fit the propeller shaft so it was thinking caps on again. We thought another gearbox would do the job. More phone calls and we set off in our bright orange Mini for Yorkshire. On the way we were stopped by the police who thought we had too much weight in the boot. When it was opened it was completely empty. We went on our way and the bonnet of the Mini came open and we almost crashed. The police hadn't shut it properly and we hadn't checked it. When we got to Yorkshire despite our enquiries we found the gearbox was nothing like the seller had said over the phone.

We decided to go and see a firm in Southampton who had several gearboxes for sale. We arrived late evening and parked off the road near some trees and decided to sleep in the car and planned to set off early next morning. It was a very cold night and the condensation built up in the car and we ended up wringing wet. We were also awoken early by the noise of things hitting the top of the car. We scrambled out and found all the acorns were falling off the large oak tree we had parked under.

We then headed for Southampton Railway Station to get a bite to eat and a wash and brush up before we continued with our mission. It was about 6am in the morning, we didn't usually bother with breakfast, but had bacon and eggs which tasted so good, we both had another helping.

We found the firm and bought another gearbox. We decided to put it in the well by the passenger seat of the Mini, it was heavier than a person but we had no option but get it back to the boat. Many hours later we arrived at our berth and when we went to get the gearbox out we noticed the tread on the nearside front tyre had 'walked' off the tyre with the weight. We were so lucky we didn't have an accident.

We had a couple of hours sleep and set to work to see if this gearbox would fit but once again it was only about an inch out so the engineering costs of altering everything would have been prohibitive. Our only option now was to throw ourselves on the mercy of Lombard, the commercial bank whom we still owed money to. We put our best gear on and headed for Llandudno to see if we could raise the funds to buy the proper engine and gearbox. We explained without the boat we would end up in arrears but given the chance we would repay all the money. We were aware we were not a good risk, the only asset was the boat which was useless with no engine. We were also water gypsies with no fixed address.

Eventually the manager agreed but said the interest rate would be the commercial rate of 25%. So be it, it was our last chance to get out of the mess we were in.

It was now November, we had spent 2 months trying to resolve our problems without going into debt but we now had to use the money wisely and find a complete engine which needed no adaptations. After many phone calls from a telephone box, (we did not have a shore line or a mobile in those days) we located an engine and a part exchange deal for the other engine.

We had to hire a wagon and load the engine on and we set off for Abingdon which meant a journey across the Welsh mountains. We set off about 2am thinking there would be little traffic. To conserve petrol our top speed was a steady 50mph, in the interests of safety and because we had quite a weight on the wagon.

We hadn't gone more than a few miles along the mountain road when we saw a stream of headlights and we seemed to be leading a convoy of vehicles, there must have been at least a dozen. They couldn't pass us as there were no passing places. We carried on for about 20 miles or more and at the first opportunity one by one they whizzed past us. Further down the road we came to a checkpoint for no other than the mountain leg of the famous Lombard Car Rally. We were signalled to pull into the layby and let the rest of the cars check in so that we wouldn't hold them up any further. The irony was that we were on our way to spend

Lombard money on the engine. We think it must have gone down in the records as the slowest mountain leg on record!!

We arrived at Abingdon, conducted our business and with the new engine secured on the wagon we set off for home. It had been a very long day. The forecast was not good as snow and ice had been forecast. We crossed the mountains again but without a convoy of cars following us. About halfway home we stopped at a pub in the middle of nowhere to get something to eat and stretch our legs. The place looked deserted but all the lights were on and we could see the glow of a log fire. We tried the door, it was unlocked and there was nobody behind the bar. We shouted and thought it strange, there was no reply and not a soul in sight. We stood for a few moments not knowing what to do. Suddenly we caught sight of a person sitting in a winged back chair. The figure slowly rose and came towards us. It was a very old lady dressed in long black clothes. If we had been drinking we would have thought we were seeing things. It was very spookie. We were quite scared. However, she did have some food for us and a cup of tea, and she was very pleasant.

Suitably refreshed we went on our way and arrived back at the boat. We were too tired to take the engine off the wagon and decided to leave it until the morning, hoping the scrap dealers would not visit in the middle of the night. Thankfully the engine was still there in the morning.

The next 4 months was full of hard slog, working late into the evening every day to install the engine. The doubting Thomas's came every day shaking heads and tut-tutting and still blaming the fact there was a woman aboard.

However in March 1976 we were ready to take the boat out on engine trials. Everything had been checked a thousand times. We waited for the tide to come in and hoped nobody would notice us leaving the quay but the jungle drums had been working overtime. We think they came to see us fail, but they were disappointed. We looked like a Chinese junk ship with all the scrap gear on deck, not at all ship shape and Bristol fashion. We proved them all wrong and the engine was still in good condition some years later when we sold the boat to get a smaller one with less maintenance. The boat earned us many a pretty penny, paid Lombard back, and was free from debt, and as far as I know she is still working for her living today.

If the boat could only tell the tale of two people, one a woman who had defied all the odds. With dogged determination against all the odds, we had completed the daunting task of putting an engine in the boat, with few resources, to win through to a happy conclusion.

March 2012

A Stitch in Time

When I was living on a boat, a fishing
trawler, down in North Wales, my
husband the skipper fell against the
bulkhead in the fo'c'sle one night and
cut his head. It was quite a nasty gash
and really needed a few stitches.
However he needed a lot of coaxing to
go to the A & E.

We eventually went to hospital and as
thought he needed three stitches.
These happened to be bright blue in
colour. The next day we were sat on
the quayside, above where our boat
was moored, in our old van, watching
the world go by.

It wasn't long before one of the fish
hawkers, who used to buy our surplus
fish which wouldn't have sold on the

open market, came along. He asked if we had any fish he could buy, when suddenly he saw that the Skipper had three bright blue stitches on his head. He asked what had happened we told him and he said, "Isn't Sylvia clever to have sewn the wound up!" Presumably he had seen us mending nets etc. and thought it was natural for us to do what was necessary without going to hospital.

After he went we couldn't stop laughing because we never told him we had been to hospital and I'm sure to this day he thinks that I had got my needle and thread out to sew the Skipper's head!!

FEATHERS

In the late 60's, I was living in Wales, and I had a young daughter aged 9 who had recently gone to the local school. This particular afternoon I was due to go to see the teachers for a progress report. I foolishly decided that I would complete a task I had started some weeks before of making a continental quilt, which were all the rage at this time.

I couldn't afford to buy one, but I had been given a feather mattress which I thought I could convert into a quilt. I had been and bought the feather-proof 'ticking' and made a single quilt cover with the necessary three pockets to put the feathers in.

I shut myself in a small bedroom complete with all the necessary materials and began the task, carefully opening the feather mattress cover and hung the quilt cover over the end of the bed. Once started there was no way of going back - handfuls of feathers were put down the relevant pockets but I hadn't realised that feathers being what they are do not stay in one place, in no time at all there were feathers everywhere. What a mess!! The more I tried to cope with the situation, the hotter I became and the smaller bits of feathers were stuck on my clothes my hair and my face, and the room was covered in a fine blanket of small feathers.

Suddenly I realised that time was up and I had to be at school I don't even remember how I managed to clean myself up to be fit to go and meet the teachers, but I just made it. I expect my face was redder than it had ever been, and I was certainly not calm and collected.

It took me weeks to clean the bedroom after I had achieved my goal of making the quilt and I vowed never again to do anything else with feathers. I often wonder would I have been better saving up to buy a ready- made one. You live and learn!!

1993

This year, my husband a trawler skipper, aged 78 yrs. passed away and as a widow I came ashore after almost 18 years living and working aboard our trawler out of Bangor, North Wales. I was 50 years old.

It was a shock to my system to say the least. I had opted out of normal society in 1975.

I was invited to stay with friends until I sorted my affairs out. They were a very successful business couple, who lived in a very large house. I lived as one of the family and was included in their lives. This was my first taste of life ashore. I was a lost soul and without their help and support I would have found it difficult to cope.

My husband had 8 children from a previous marriage who were all of my generation. They rallied round and between them they agreed to contribute to the funeral costs. I had very little in the way of funds as we hadn't worked for a couple of years because of my husband's illness. So far so good.

It wasn't long before I was told that two of them wouldn't pay and that the boat was legally theirs. There was no will and I had to apply for Letters of Administration to be able to sort out the affairs and state my claim to the boat. My friend had influence and my claim was confirmed as valid in two weeks. Quite a record as it often takes months when someone dies without a will.

I needed to buy some suitable clothes for the funeral but only had limited funds. My clothing was only suitable for a boat. Time was short so my friend took me to Llandudno and straight to M & S for underwear, black trousers and a top. She was a regular customer there and she just clicked her fingers and staff came running and were asked to take measurements. I had no idea what size I was. Purchases were made which took quite a bit of my meagre savings.

The next place to go was a shoe shop. It was an old fashioned shop with staff to match, and I wondered if I could afford the shoes. I was wearing my friend's shoes which were a size 6. The Staff were very attentive and one of the older male assistants was dispatched to bring a variety of shoes. The shop was very long with steps halfway down and the storeroom was in the basement. After about ten minutes the assistant came back, out of breath, with a selection of different styles.

I was getting quite agitated as it was the first shopping expedition I had been involved in for many years. I was told to take my socks off and put on a 'pop' sock (something I had never heard of). I was wearing three pairs of socks, the norm for living on a boat in winter time, there was a gasp and my friend said in shock and amazement "You've only got little feet!"

The assistant was sent away again to bring the correct size. Away he went down the shop, down the steps and into the basement and came running back with another selection of shoes. It was like a sketch from a farce. You couldn't have made it up. My friend took it all in her stride, I nearly collapsed laughing at the situation. Needless to say I came out of it with only a few pounds left.

The funeral was looming, the undertaker was a friend of my surrogate family so he had been instructed to provide his very best hearse a Rolls Royce for the journey to Anfield Cemetery in Liverpool. I expect the skipper was looking down in amazement. His comments would have been unrepeatable!!

The day arrived, which ironically happened to be Red Nose Day. There was to be a graveside service by the Chaplain of the Port of Liverpool a simple service with a few readings. On the way I looked out over the water on

the coast road and poignantly there
was a beautiful rainbow in the sky.

The family had wanted him to be buried
at sea but he had told me he didn't
want that so I decided to put him with
his mother and father which was not
controversial. We arrived and met up
with my family who came to support
me. His family were all congregated at
the bottom of the plot. Nobody spoke
to me, they all just stared, despite
having been accepted by them over the
years. I think these occasions bring the
bad out in people.

The two sons had enormous black
overcoats on and they looked like
gangsters. You could have cut the air
with a knife. My father was quite
worried and took no chances and
positioned himself with his back to a

tree. There was a lot of tension nobody knew it wasn't going to 'kick off'. There were about 100 people there, many from the fishing fraternity. He had been a very special person a fisherman for nearly 50 years and very well respected.

Once the service was over everyone from my side beat a hasty retreat as there was no 'do' afterwards.

I now had to start a new chapter in my life. I knew it would be difficult as I now had to integrate back into the big world outside after nearly 20 years of being a water gypsy.

Sylvia Sharples

IRONY IN DEATH

A few years ago my mother and I were both widowed in the same year. When arranging my husband's funeral, it was complicated as he had a grown up family who were about my age. I was staying with friends in Wales, and the funeral was arranged, believe it or not for Red Nose Day. My friend asked if I wanted a red rose to put in the grave – (red rose for red nose day). The irony was unbelievable, and it just broke the ice. He was taken in a Rolls Royce hearse, the best transport available.

On arrival for the graveside ceremony, at the foot of the grave were his children and ex-wife, the men wearing long dark overcoats, all spread out in a line, it looked like a scene from the Godfather. My father positioned himself with his back to a tree as he thought something might happen. It didn't – but we all made a swift exit when the ceremony was over.

A few months later my father passed away. On the way to the crematorium we were lead by a refuse wagon with the word "Vulture" on the back. Mother saw the funny side of this. After his funeral, a couple came up and thanked my mother for a lovely service, they had really enjoyed it – but they thought it was another person's funeral with the same name!

I was living with my mother – as we had both been recently widowed - the mix-ups with phone calls regarding inscriptions on graves and memorials were very hard to believe. Truth is stranger than fiction! At times it was

like a theatre farce. You had to have a
sense of humour to get through that
dark period. The old adage, laughter is
only a hair's breadth from crying was
very true on these occasions.

May 2011

MINT TEA

This story occurred in 1994, a few months after I had come ashore after spending 18 yrs. living and working aboard a trawler until my husband passed away. I was now living with my mother who was also recently widowed. Two widows in one house does have its ups and downs.

One day I noticed an advert in the local paper which read "Boat sitter wanted". I still had a yearning to be on the water so rang the guy and he asked me to meet him at the canal basin in Ashton under Lyne where he was renovating a large barge for the Canal Boat Trust.

In my possession I had a box full of very large spanners and boat tools which I now had no use for, so I took these with me. He was delighted as these tools are very expensive to buy new. I was glad I had found a good home for them.

He welcomed me aboard, gave me a history of the barge and said it was being refurbished ready to carry cargo down through the canals to the South of England. A team of Trust volunteers would work in relays along the route some using a week of their holidays others for longer and the 'boat sitter' was needed to stay aboard whilst the crew changed over. The cargo was tons of cobblestones for a guy who had bought them from a dealer in this area.

He showed me the accommodation which was quite small in comparison to the size of the barge. He said a whole family would have slept and eaten here in the past. There was a pot belly stove, a tiny sink, and a cupboard which turned out to be the sleeping quarters. He said it was called a 'bed-hole', not a bunk as on other boats.

He said that I would need to be able to walk along the top plank of the barge, jump to the next boat if there was a queue at the lock gates, ready to take my turn on the lock gate handle. He arranged to phone me and take me to Runcorn the next week to see his smaller barge and another one belonging to the Trust which I could have if I wanted to refurbish it.

So far so good, I was very interested but wasn't sure about leaping from barge to barge but he assured me it was quite easy! The plank along the top is about 3ins thick and 14ins wide.

Canals are quite shallow, but I didn't fancy a mouthful of the dirty water.

He collected me from my mothers in a very dilapidated car and we set off for the canal in Runcorn. Every time we stopped at lights he switched the engine off which I thought very odd, but he said it saved on petrol.

We arrived at the cutting where his boat was moored, it was in the middle of nowhere, with several barges all in different states of repair, not one of them appeared to be working. He took me to see the spare barge which was just a hull, requiring fitting out. It was about 65ft long made of steel, but too big a task for me to take on.

He showed me how to climb aboard, there just being enough room along the covered cargo area to put your toes on and then to climb on to the top plank, nothing to hold onto. It was very precarious. However, I managed to stand upright and make my leap of faith onto the next barge. He congratulated me and said I had passed the test.

We went back to his barge and gave me a lecture about not buying Nestle products, due to child labour being involved. He asked if I would like a cup of tea, and did I like mint tea? I declined and he no more than jumped off the barge ran onto the tow path and grabbed a handful of mint! He threw it into the teapot and made tea. I was flabbergasted, but kept my cool and had normal tea. He had brought aboard a bag containing vegetables which he had rescued from a bin at the greengrocers, cut all the bad off and proceeded to make stew.

We talked about boats and ourselves for a couple of hours, until the stew was ready. He had been an academic, had opted out of society and his marriage after losing his only disabled daughter, and had thrown himself into the work of the Trust. I tasted the stew and it was remarkably good much to my surprise.

By now time had moved on and it was about 9.30pm so I asked when he would be taking me back home. He said he was staying there as it was his home. My heart sank and I said I had to get back to look after my mother who would be getting very worried by now. I asked if there was a bus or train to Manchester. He dug around and found a tatty timetable. He said he would take me to the station which was about 10mins away.

On arrival on the platform, there was a large gang of teenage youths and I was quite worried so asked if he would wait until the train came. I didn't know if I had enough money for the ticket but thought I'd sort that out when the ticket man came. It was a local train and seemed to take for ever to get to Manchester. I then had to catch the tram to Altrincham, and just managed to catch the last tram. Whew – I've never been so relieved. I ran like the wind and was shaking like a leaf when I arrived home. What an ordeal all self-inflicted just because of my love of boats. I vowed then to find out the facts before embarking on any hair brained scheme. I should have known better but there's no fool like an old fool, and I wasn't even street wise.

I never became a boat sitter and I often wonder if the cobblestones ever reached their destination, and I didn't even ring up to find out, I realised I was well out of my depth.

March 2012

THE PRESENCE

 In the late 1990's I was trading in an old building which had been converted into market stalls, like a flea market or bazaar. It was a very colourful place full of stalls selling everything from retro to punk. People from all walks of life used to visit to take in the atmosphere and wander round amazed at the variety of goods and services on sale.

I had been aware for some time that there was an aura about the place, especially in the older part of the building. Sometimes I could feel a presence but nothing to be frightened of. I had experienced this kind of thing for most of my life at certain times and in certain places.

The story I am about to tell started one night as I was closing my shop and members of the public had left. I heard the rustle of taffeta and a strong smell of camphor reminiscent of Victorian or Edwardian days I had read about. I felt that this presence was very agitated and cross about something. On the way home I thought about what had happened.

The next day I noticed a new shop was being fitted out and was curious to know what would be on sale. The guy, who was in his late thirties, told me, when I asked, that he was going to sell books on the supernatural, crystals, talisman, herbal remedies, special stones with healing properties etc. He also said he was going to do a daily horoscope which he would obtain from his computer and put it on a white board on an easel every day at 12 noon. He said he would also give private readings for people who wanted something a bit more special.

All went well for the first week. A crowd would gather waiting for the 12 noon forecasts and he seemed to be pleased with the trade he was generating. One morning as I passed his stall I saw him painting something on the wall, I looked and it was a pentagon! That's not good I thought, and I asked why he was doing it. He said to give the place more authenticity. I said "I hope you know what you are doing putting that sign on the wall". He said he knew what he was doing, we had a bit of banter and I left it at that.

At 12 noon the crowd gathered waiting for the horoscope but he had to tell them that his computer was playing up and couldn't seem to get the forecast. He was very embarrassed but apologised and told them he would make sure there would be a horoscope the next day. The next morning, there were groups of stall holders talking about strange things which had happened overnight throughout the building. Items from one shop had ended up in another, one trader found a rail full of clothes had been placed folded up in the centre of their shop and water had been sprinkled round in a circle, but the clothes weren't wet or damaged. This was unexplainable. I went to my shop and there in the middle of the floor were several boxes of footwear, which had been on a shelf high up, they hadn't fallen down, the boxes still had the lids on. How strange, I began to think of the 'presence' I had felt and the agitated feeling I experienced. The place was buzzing with theories and the usual comments from the sceptics.

That night as I was getting ready to close my shop, I went to the shop opposite which I had been minding for that day. This shop had some of the double sided mirrors which hung in a stand so it could be reversed. The place was deserted as it was the end of the day, when all of a sudden one mirror turned slowly over on its own. Next thing I heard the rustle of taffeta and a very strong smell of camphor. I heard or thought I heard a whisper which said "Get rid of that pentagon". I wasn't surprised as I my instinct had told me that the outline of a pentagon wasn't a good thing.

The next day, I spoke to the guy and told him he didn't know what he was playing with or what he was evoking and the "presence" was not at all pleased with the pentagon in his shop. He said he was only trying to make a living.

The strange happenings continued, the horoscopes were hit and miss, no continuity, eventually people got fed up of waiting. The computer forecasts were still unreliable, and it wasn't long before the guy shut up shop for lack of funds. As soon as the shop was empty, someone got some paint and a brush, and obliterated the pentagon.

That same night I had one more visit from the 'presence', I felt something glide past me, I heard a slight rustle of taffeta and the feint aroma of camphor. There seemed to be a calm and serenity about it this time. The agitation and anger had gone.

I wondered was the presence the guardian of the building or was it a figment of my imagination? I don't think so, these things had happened, and I saw them with my own eyes, as did other traders whose goods had been moved around. Truth is stranger than fiction as the old adage goes!!

February 2011

WEDDING DIGNATORIES

Some 10 years ago a young man and his bride to be, moved into a house in our street and despite our age differences we all got on very well together. Their wedding date had been set and we were duly invited to the evening reception which was being held in Oldham.

The day arrived and we dressed in our best bib and tuckers and eventually found our way to the reception. I had my long evening dress on and my husband his best suit and waistcoat. After introductions to their families, we settled down for the evening. Everyone was extremely courteous and exchanged pleasantries with us.

When my husband went to join the
queue at the bar everyone stepped
aside and let him go to the front of the
queue. We thought it very strange, not
the norm where beer is concerned!
This behaviour continued throughout
the evening.

When the celebrations were over our
hosts arranged transport for us to go to
the house where we were to spend the
night. We chatted and thanked them
for a good evening. My husband
commented about everyone letting him
go to the front of the queue. The
groom said he had a confession to
make. He said he had told his guests
that he had invited some special people
to the reception. They asked who it
was and he had told them it was the
Lord Mayor and Lady Mayoress of
Salford. Obviously they hadn't believed

him until we turned up dressed as we were. They asked him how he had such influential connections.

We burst out laughing because it explained the behaviour of the other guests whenever my husband went to the bar. He was a practical joker and we often smile when we think of that night.

I we had known the truth during the evening it would have been hard to keep up the sham. Good job we were totally unaware and we had dressed appropriately for dignitaries, or his joke would have back fired.

July 2012

ARTICLES

A SIDEWAYS VIEW OF ORDSALL

Some 9 years ago we came to live in Ordsall. We had been living in private accommodation in Stretford, the landlord was going to sell the house and we had to find somewhere to live within a month. Friends had told us of a Council estate in in Ordsall which was run by the tenants who were looking for people who wanted to be involved in a community.

We were interviewed and accepted on the waiting list and very soon a house was offered to us. We couldn't believe our luck but were full of trepidation moving to a new area not knowing anyone and having to start all over again with both of us over half a century old!!

The only times we had been to Ordsall was for a Country and Western theme day at this estate which we had thoroughly enjoyed. The other time was another country and western night at the community centre/youth club on Craven Drive.

The latter had proved very difficult to get a taxi back to Stretford. Nobody from the Stretford taxi firms would come and pick us up. We were all dressed up, it was almost midnight, we were ridiculed and heckled by passers-by and Salford taxi drivers alike. We must have looked a strange trio, two men dressed as the Earp brothers and me as a cowgirl. The mind boggles. However, we did eventually after many

phone calls get back to Stretford
(phew!)

We moved into our new home,
squeezing the contents of a large 3 bed
terrace into a much smaller place. The
two removal men seemed to spend
more time drinking tea. The 'van' (if
you could call it that), was a large
Transit and a trailer, the owner a very
small guy full of wit and his 'mate' was
a gentle giant of a man who was
ordered about by the 'boss' who just
sat on the only kitchen chair directing
operations - think we did more lifting
and carrying than they did. Good job
we could see the funny side of it. The
'boss's' final parting shot to me was
'next time you move – don't ring me I'll
ring you!'

It wasn't long before people made offers of help if we needed any and not be shy about asking – a true community spirit which I hadn't experienced since I lived with my parents as a child. It felt like coming home.

We soon got involved with events run by the co-operative and served on some of the committees, everyone is encouraged to volunteer an hour or so a week, without such participation the co-op would cease to be.

There are some minor problems in the community but the area is undergoing big changes, which takes time to absorb. Salford Lads Club has received heritage status and there is talk that our estate could be included. These houses were built at the turn of the 1900's, the first social housing in Salford. At the moment they are undergoing a major refurbishment to decent homes standards. My grandfather lived in one of the back to back houses somewhere near our medical centre, according to the 1881 census, so I have come back to my roots – what a small world!

Credit should be given to the people who fought to keep these houses and to make it a good area to live. They put up with many setbacks before setting up the New Barracks Tenants Management Co-operative, run by the people for the people. Without them who knows where we would have ended up living.

There is so much going on in the Ordsall area if you want to get involved. Ordsall Community Arts holds lots of events, Gail Skelly works tirelessly for this community, especially the highlight of the year, The Festival of Light and the Ordsall Festival. Ordsall Acapella Singers started off at OCA and now has a 40 strong choir who perform at various venues in Salford and beyond. This year they are appearing at the Buxton Musical Festival. They have been on the television and local radio programmes.

The Community Café is another hive of activity, this also is run mainly by volunteers who put a lot of energy providing facilities for toddlers' groups, computer courses, hairdressing, bingo and of course good food at reasonable prices. Stacy the manager works hard to organise events at the café, writing newsletters, raising funds for projects and informing the local community of events that take place in the many rooms above the café.

I attended many sessions in the IT suite which opened up a whole new world where I discovered I had the ability to write articles for newsletters or reports on local events. This led to participation in the recent Creative Writing sessions where I composed my first ever poems – another surprise to myself and others.

If I hadn't come to live in Ordsall I doubt if I would have had this kind of opportunity to belong to a community. I have made many acquaintances and friends over the past 9 years and hope I too have contributed to the area, even if it's only the fun I have had in writing reports on the activities in the hope it would encourage others to come along and join in.

So – despite my misgivings about moving here, I think Ordsall is a wonderful place to live and feel I have come to the end of a few of my personal memories of the past 9 years when such a lot of things have happened and opportunities taken. All credit must go to the people who made it possible, and the tremendous hard work which goes on daily to help this community bond together. Thanks!

May 2010

ORDSALL FESTIVAL 20th SEPTEMBER 2008

What a change - the weather was fine and dry – and as they say the sun shines on the righteous!!

A lot of time and effort had been put into organizing the event Gail Skelly in particular was the co-ordinator and rushed around the various performers telling them when they would be on stage.

There were so many groups almost all from the Ordsall area and local talent was prolific – if only their enthusiasm had been matched by the attendance of people from the area. Most of the support was from friends and families of the performers.

However, the day went well, we had a samba band and the Kidswidreams danced to the music, there were, Congolese dancers, belly dancers, hip hop and rap dancers, acapella singers, some groups performing twice. The atmosphere was full of brightly coloured outfits which represented the different cultures.

There were quite a few stalls, - One was showing children how to make use of old plastic bags and using them to make craft items. The Refuse Department were there with information regarding the new litter bins, and showing the items which are not recyclable. Ross Spanner manned the Friends of Ordsall Park stall, and Mike and Jane had a stall about Salford's past and retracing Salford.

Ordsall Community Café were serving food in one of the marquees with their volunteer helpers. St Clements Church had a cake stall and tombola stall. The Seedley & Langworthy in Bloom group were showing people what can be achieved by community involvement in their local area to plant flowers and grow some home produce.

The last stall I visited was the remarkable story of the Sioux Indians who came to Salford with Buffalo Bills Wild West Show in 1887 and camped on the banks of the Irwell. There is still a link to their community in Dakota. There were artifacts to see and a craft stall with a Sioux theme for making masks etc. for the grand parade at the end of the event.

The bouncy castle didn't quite happen – they had left their safety certificate in Middlesbrough so were unable to set it up.

It was a very good day but there needs to be more advertising next time and more support from group leaders and businesses in the area, who could attend and support the local groups working so hard to bring all age groups and cultures together. We all need to work together to make this happen and not leave it to the few who are already working so hard to benefit the area. Bring back the community spirit!!

Community Reporter

TOUR OF THE BBC STUDIOS IN MANCHESTER
Wednesday 23rd April 2008

Information regarding these tours was sent to us by Alison Cordingley of the Community Café, Ordsall. We booked our tour on-line and had to be at the BBC on Oxford Road at 10am.

On arrival we were issued with passes with our names and waited for Anne Rabbitt, who was conducting the tours, to arrive and take us on our conducted tour. Our first call was made at Studio 'A' which is the largest studio and where many past series were filmed, but it is not used very often now. It is available to hire to various film companies, but they would have to provide all their own lighting and equipment. Life on Mars was filmed here when the police station set was made and apparently, staff from the BBC was always bumping into figures dressed in 70's clothing, popping in and out of make-up and dressing rooms. The bright red Cortina was also parked in the car park at the back of the building.

We were shown dressing rooms, not glamorous at all, very basic with a couple of easy chairs, a TV, and a very small en suite shower/bathroom. We were told stars very often order their own special request items, which they pay for. The make-up room was also very basic, more like something from the 70's together with a very small hairdressing room. Also on site is the costume department where artists go to be fitted with their outfits, this is equipped with sewing machines etc.

We then went to see the studio of the BBC Philharmonic Orchestra where they were in full "tuning up mode". We waited in the shadows listening to the cacophony of sound, all went quiet and the conductor brought them to order and they began their rehearsal. It was very moving. There are at the most 120 musicians playing and the full rehearsals can be watched by the public at specified times, but booking is essential. Sessions are all free, so you just have to ring and book to attend. So come on all you classical music fans, they usually take place in the afternoons, so could appeal to those not wanting to go out at night. We crept out whilst they were still playing and went to see the radio drama section.

This studio was amazing and the young lady who took us round and explained everything was very informative.

There is a carpeted area, a completely soundproofed small room where all the dialogue is spoken and it apparently sounds like the outdoors, also three sets of stairs leading no-where! The three give different effects when the actors run up and down them. There isn't a dressing room as the actors wear their own clothes as it is not being filmed. The Archers used to be broadcast from this studio.

There are a lot of dramas on the various BBC programmes which are all made here. Sound effects are added after the recording from a data base on the computer. Since technology has improved, all the BBC sound effects have taken a year to put on the data base. This means the studio team do not have to be as innovative as they were in the past to create effects.

Our last studio was North West Tonight, which has changed since I was there a year ago. We saw the famous settees where Gordon Burns sits and had our photographs taken there. We saw Heather Stott behind a glass screen broadcasting on Radio Manchester, she waved to us and said hello! We were told that all the presenters and team of the North West studio do all their own 'ops' (they have an earpiece and take instructions from the director). In the gallery overlooking the studio is the technical side of all the live performances with banks of monitors and goodness knows how many switches, last minute changes and news flashes are all controlled from there.

This was the first of the tours organised by the BBC, and they are in the process of setting up a studio which will be interactive. There will be a chance to read the news and give a weather forecast, obviously not on air, but simulated so you can watch it afterwards. This could be of great interest to young people who are thinking of a career in the media whether on the technical side or the presenting side.

All in all it was very interesting and the tours have been particularly aimed at residents of Salford prior to the move to Salford Quays, so that local residents can see behind the scenes of the BBC before it moves. When they move, there are going to be lots of different TV companies in the same development and all will have to pre-book the specialist studios which are going to be available. The BBC Philharmonic Orchestra are going to have their own studio, as now, and they are hoping that the acoustics will be as good if not better than the one they now occupy.

Sylvia Sharples
Community Reporter,
Ordsall Community Cafe

FICTION

PRIORITIES

Jack trudged home from school through the woods. It was autumn and the leaves were thick on the ground. He loved the "swish swish" as he moved through them. It was comforting, and the smell of nature conjured up all sorts of emotions.

School was somewhere he'd rather not be. He struggled with reading and writing and found it hard to concentrate on lessons. He would drift off to places far away. He had heard tales of adventure from the seamen down on the quay. He wished he was older so he could sail away to these far flung places. He vowed one day he would become a seaman and visit all these places and come back and talk to his friends about his travels.

As soon as the bell for the end of lessons sounded he was first out of school, he would think about all sorts of things on the way home. He wished he could help his mother more, she had found it hard since his father died. She had been lucky to find a cleaning job, times were hard, for everybody. His route took him through the woods and down into the village where there were several small shops, one of which was the grocer's store owned by Mr. Diggle.

This day, when he passed the grocer's shop, Mr.Diggle had a notice in the window, and he could just about read the offer of a job. He went in the shop and asked what the job was. Mr.Diggle said it was delivering groceries, but that he would need a bike to do this. His heart sank, he knew they couldn't afford to buy even a second hand bike.

He carried on walking home, he knew his mother would be waiting by the window, she would be back from her cleaning job, exhausted and still in mourning a year on from the loss of his father.

She had taken any job to provide for them both, there were no benefits available in those days. A person had to sell most of their possessions before they would be considered destitute. She had been interviewed by the Board of Guardians who told her she did not qualify for assistance, so had had to go and find some kind of work.

Jack was determined to help, and had been and asked the more affluent neighbours if he could run messages for them and received the odd penny here and there. This was not really enough, if only he could take this job at Mr. Diggles's. How could he get a bike he wondered? Any old bike would do. Suddenly he remembered seeing a rusty old bike up in the woods but had forgotten about it, he had never given it a second thought until now.

He ate his tea and told his mother he wanted to go out and play. She said it was ok but he should come back before dark. He was so excited, he ran all the way to the woods and managed to drag the rusty old bike out of the grass. He couldn't believe his luck, it was still there and could be the answer to his prayers. He realised he would need help to make it useable but he had to take it home first as it was getting dark and his mother would be worried about him. He thought he would ask Joe, a neighbour who lived a few doors down, if he could help him. Joe had been out of work for some time, he had worked in one of the factories, but had been laid off as there was no work.

He carried the bike home, whereupon his mother accused him of stealing the bike. "No!" he said "I found it in the bushes in the woods". She looked at him as if she didn't believe him. "Honestly!" he said. When she looked at the bike she realised it had long since been abandoned. He said "Can I go and ask Joe if he can help me to repair it?" She said, "Don't be mithering Joe too much, he's been very good to us since your father died, and we don't want to

take advantage of people." "Okay" said
Jack, "But can I go and ask him now?"
"Alright, she said, but don't be long, I
need you to help with some jobs in the
house".

He went and asked Joe if he could help
him to repair an old bike, and told Joe
why it was so important, because of the
chance of working for Mr. Diggle. Joe
said "Bring it here and I'll have a look at
it, I can't promise anything, but we'll
see if we can do something with it." "I'll
bring it to you after school tomorrow."
said Jack.

He told his mother Joe was going to
help him to repair the bike, but not the
reason why he wanted it so
desperately. He found it hard to sleep
that night, all sorts of thoughts
rushing through his head. Next

morning, he felt as if he hadn't slept all night. At school he kept dozing off, and was in trouble more than once. The day dragged until at last the bell rang for the end of lessons. He didn't dawdle on the way home, he ran like the wind, arriving home well out of breath. His mother wasn't home yet – "Good" – he thought, I can take my bike to Joe's house.

Jack took the bike to Joe's house. Joe was secretly glad to be able to do something for the lad, after all it wouldn't cost any money, only time. It would also give him something to do, he had been feeling down in the dumps recently not being able to find any work. At least he could try and help Jack. They looked at the bike together, it seemed a hopeless task, but Joe had the heart of a lion and said "I think we can do something with it. You can help me and I'll show you what to do." They worked together until late in the evening. Jack needed the bike by Saturday so they had two days left to complete the work. Joe fashioned some parts out of odds and ends he had in his shed and slowly the bike was renovated. The transformation was amazing.

Thursday night came and the finishing touches were added and a somewhat rusty bike now had a new coat of paint and was able to be ridden, brakes working and a framework on the handlebars to carry the orders. Jack's face beamed - at last he could help his mother she hadn't looked very well recently - she had been working too hard.

Jack took the bike home and put it in the yard covering it with an old piece of carpet, there was nowhere else to keep it. He went to school the next day, and found it even more difficult to listen to his lessons. He was thinking of his bike and hoping that Mr. Diggle hadn't given the job to someone else. The day dragged on until the final bell went for the end of lessons. At last he could call and tell Mr.Diggle that he now had a bike and could he have the job.

He arrived at the grocers out of breath but full of excitement. Mr. Diggle had gone out, his wife was in the shop and she told Jack he would have to come back in an hour when her husband was in. Time seemed to crawl at a snail's pace, " How long was an hour?" Jack had no idea, he couldn't even tell the time, and didn't even own a watch. He went up to some of his class mates who were standing on the corner. He didn't want to tell them why he hadn't gone straight home in case one of them wanted the job advertised in the grocer's shop window. He told them his mother was still at work and there was no need to go home until later.

After what he thought was an hour he went back to Mr. Diggles's shop and saw that he had returned. He rushed in and could hardly get the words out – telling Mr. Diggle he now had a bike and could he still have the job. Mr.Diggle was pleased to see how determined Jack was and thought he would be a reliable person to deliver the orders. He said "Right – come down in the morning at 9 o'clock and I'll have some orders ready for you to deliver. Don't be late - mind you.

People expect their groceries on time!" "Alright Mr. Diggle, I won't let you down. I need to earn some money to help my mother. "Yes" Mr. Diggle said, "I know how hard it's been since you lost your father. It's a good job your mother has you to look out for her, she hasn't been looking so well recently". "No Jack said, I'm very worried about her, she's working too hard. I just want to help." See you in the morning then Jack – and don't be late". "Thanks Mr. Diggle, I'll be here before time." Jack left the shop and Mr. Diggle said to his wife, "That lad's a credit to Mary, they brought him up properly. If I had a son I would hope he was like Jack". "Yes!" his wife said, "but it wasn't meant to be, I'm sorry we didn't have any children".

Jack rushed home, he was on top of the world, he'd managed to get a Saturday job, he couldn't believe his luck. His mother wasn't home, which was unusual. He was quite worried, where could she be, he hoped nothing had happened to her. He busied himself, washed the few dishes which were in the sink, put the kettle on the hob and waited for what seemed ages. Mary came home, Jack was relieved, all sorts of things go through your head when someone isn't there when they should be. It was more frightening especially after the loss of his father. He didn't want to be alone in the world.

He told his mother that the bike was finished and the reason why he wanted it so much. He could now work for Mr. Diggle on a Saturday morning and earn some money for them.

His mother looked unwell, she asked him to make her a cup of tea and said she had something to tell him. He wondered what it could be, she looked really upset. He sat down on the stool by her and he could see she was struggling for words.

She began "Jack I don't know how to tell you this, but I sold your bike today." His heart sank and he thought, "How could you?" He waited for her to continue, anger was building inside, but he had been brought up not to answer back. She said, "I haven't been very well, and I needed some money to pay the doctor for some medicine, there was no way I could earn enough to keep us and pay for a doctor. Jack I'm really really sorry. I know how much you wanted to help."

Jack was devastated, his hopes were shattered, he would now have to go and tell Mr. Diggle, he couldn't take the job. Mr. Diggle's customers wouldn't get the deliveries they were expecting, he had let people down. Mr Diggle understood but said to Jack "I'm afraid it's a lesson in life son, your priorities in life aren't necessarily the same as someone elses."

Later on in life Jack realised, that when he had tried to help his mother, he had succeeded but not in the way he thought. If he hadn't found the bike, his mother wouldn't have been able to sell it and get the help she needed. Life is full of disappointments and lessons to learn.

January 2011

LOVE

Claire who was in her mid-30's had been on her own for some time due to circumstances – elderly parents, and a full time career. There was no chance of meeting anyone only at work. She had heard people talking about meeting someone on the internet but not all had turned out successful.

This particular evening she decided to look on her Hotmail Account and see if they had something like that. She thought if she clicked on the icon it didn't mean she had to sign up. A few moments later she plucked up the courage and decided it was worth a try. She filled in the details and waited. Soon there were all kinds of people wanting to be contacted. She browsed through the photos and profiles and picked two out.

Over the next few weeks she chatted on line to both, one was called Carl and the other Tony. She got to know them quite well, and decided that Tony would be the one she wanted to meet. She was very apprehensive but arranged to meet Tony in a public place, just as the guidelines said.

When she arrived a few minutes early, she noticed a guy standing in a doorway with a small bunch of flowers in his hand. He seemed much older than the photo, but she didn't make the first move she just waited for him to make contact. Her nerves were in a state, she had never done anything like this before. She wanted to run away but held her cool.

The guy came over and asked if she was Claire and asked her to go for a coffee at the nearby café. They walked together both feeling very comfortable in each other's company. They talked over coffee when Claire realised Tony's face was familiar, she remembered him from when she was at school. He would be about 4 years older than her. He seemed to always be on his own at break time and she had felt sorry for him.

After they had spent a couple of hours chatting, they went their separate ways and arranged to meet the next week. He took her to a show and they really enjoyed each other's company. They continued the pattern of meeting once a week and they would go to the cinema or for a meal. Claire felt herself getting more involved, but was still afraid of being hurt, she realised that he probably felt the same.

Next time they met she would tell him of her feelings and her fear of being hurt. She told him her fears and he confessed he felt the same. She told him how she had remembered him from school. He laughed and together they wondered if fate had taken a hand. They realised they were in love and he put his arm round her, kissed her tenderly and they both said at the same time, how glad they had met and it was all thanks to Hotmail.

February 2011

THE GNOMES

The Little boy whose name was Tobias ·
(Toby for short) looked out of the
window and saw the rain pouring
down. "I won't be able to play out
today", he said to himself.

He loved playing in the garden and
talking to the garden gnomes who were
always keeping watch in the garden.
He knew they were only made of stone,
but he played make-believe in his head
and gave them names.

There was Sebastian, the largest gnome
of all. He had brightly coloured painted
clothes and he seemed to have a glint
in his eye. Next to him were several
smaller ones, who reminded him of
little elves, and could have come from a
land faraway. Then there was the one

with the wheelbarrow called Caracas, who looked at home among the plants, and had a kindly old face.

One day he began to wonder what would happen if they all came alive just for a day. What a good time they could have! He made a wish every night before going to sleep, that his garden friends could come to life and talk to him. He never told anyone about his wish. He'd heard grown-ups say that wishes should be kept secret or they wouldn't come true.

He went every day to see the gnomes hoping some magic had happened. Then, one day, he thought he saw Sebastian wink at him. He looked again and Sebastian spoke "Hello Toby – how are you?" He was a bit frightened but said "I'm fine, how are you?" Sebastian said, "Would you help me and carry me to the other side of the garden, it's so cold here I would like to feel the sun on my face". Toby looked to see if there were any grown-ups about. There was nobody around so he carried Sebastian to the other side of the garden. "Thank you", said Sebastian, "But don't get into trouble or tell anyone I asked you to move me". "Okay." said Toby. "How long do you want to stay there for?" "Just 'til tonight when the sun goes down" said Sebastian.

Toby ran round the garden leaping and shouting, so happy that his wish had come true. As soon as the sun went down he crept down to the garden, and carried Sebastian back to his usual place. "Thanks." said Sebastian "That has really cheered me up."

It wasn't long before Caracas with the wheelbarrow spoke to him. "Will you take me near the pond I would like to meet the frogs who live there. I like the croaking noises they make and love to watch them leaping around. I want to be by the pond I don't like the flower bed, it's too quiet". Toby said, "Maybe the grown-ups won't notice if I leave you here". "Thanks" said Caracas, "My wish has come true as well".

He then went to see the tiny group of gnomes who all spoke to him at once. He had named them The Elves. They seemed to speak in another language. "Where are you from?" Toby asked. They could speak in English as well so they said, "we're from Norway and want to ask you to help us to go back home, we don't' like it here". Toby said, "I'm sorry I don't know where Norway is". "It's near the North Pole", they all shouted. He thought for a few minutes and said, "I may be able to help, I will write to Santa Clause, who lives near the North Pole but you will have to wait until Christmas". "Okay", they all said. "We'll wait - after all a few more months won't matter we've been here for years already".

Toby's friendship with all his garden friends made him very happy. Soon it was December and time for writing the letter to Santa at the North Pole. He wrote and begged Santa to call on his way past his house and take his friends back to their homeland in Norway and that would be the best present he could ever have.

When Christmas morning arrived, he opened his presents, he then put his warm clothes on as it had been snowing hard. His Mum told him to put his wellingtons on as well. He couldn't control his excitement as he plodded down the garden path. To his delight he saw an empty space in the snow and the tiny gnomes were no longer there. Santa must have given them a lift back home where they belonged. "Who said Santa wasn't real". He said to himself.

The Elves weren't missed until the Spring. The grown-ups were saying, "Where have they gone who could have stolen them?" Toby knew, this was his special secret, to be kept forever. He talked to Sebastian and Caracas whenever he could. They were quite happy in their places in the garden. They both told him The Elves asked them to say "Thank you", on their behalf.

Toby soon grew up and his visits to talk to the gnomes grew less as school work and other things became more important. His parents one day told him they had sold the house and they would be moving to a new home soon. He asked if the gnomes would be moving too. "No", they said we're leaving them for the children who are coming to live here.

He went one last time to see Sebastian and Caracas and told them there would be another boy and girl coming to look after them. They said goodbye to each other, and said they would all miss each other.

Years later when he had a family of his own, he would tell his children a bedtime story about gnomes who talked to special people. They loved

every minute of the story and he had to
tell it over and over again. He never
told them it was him who had helped
all the gnomes - that would be his
secret for ever!

March 2011

BIOGRAPHY

A BRIEF GLIMPSE OF MY LIFE

I was born during the war in North Manchester. My mother came from Patricroft and her father came from Ireland in 1870. Recently I found him on the 1881 Census living in Ordsall off Robert Hall Street, only a stone's throw from where I live now!

I had a happy childhood but not good health. I was told I couldn't do everything other kids did or I would be ill. I was always in trouble for not obeying.

We had family holidays in the Isle of Man with my parents and siblings. How

Mum managed to save up for these I will never know - times were really difficult then. I loved the ferry crossings and all my spending money I saved was spent on fishing trips, dipping for mackerel with hand lines. It was my greatest treat.

I eventually passed through school gaining some GCE's and took a secretarial course at the Manchester College of Commerce, passing with flying colours.

On leaving college I found work in the Trustee Department of Williams Deacons Bank. (now the Royal Bank of Scotland). I found the work a little bit depressing as it was dealing with wills and people's effects and last wishes.

My next job was in an advertising
agency working as secretary to one of
the directors. He had come from a
theatre background, his mother was
the daughter of a well- known music
hall star. Life was never dull there was
always something going on. Whilst
working here I had met my husband to
be. It was in the early 60's and
recession had set in, resulting in my
future husband being laid off work and
having to find another job just 6 weeks
before we were to be married.

He applied for many jobs as a
draughtsman but wasn't successful,
until the week before the wedding and
he gained employment in Sheffield.
This meant we would have to find
somewhere to live and I would have to
leave work in Manchester and move to
Yorkshire. It was a very difficult time.

We set up home in Sheffield and eventually my daughter was born, but money was still very tight. The situation vacant columns were scoured for any jobs back in Manchester. He eventually found a job in Duckinfield so we moved back across the border and lived in the front parlour of his father's house. My daughter was only a few months old but I had to look after the whole family, my husband, his sister and father. I had to do all the household chores, cooking, cleaning, shopping etc. I found it very exhausting, I was only 21 so it was a big responsibility. However I managed to obey all the rules and keep up with things.

I decided that this wasn't the life for me and vowed I would go back to work when my daughter was old enough to be left with a child minder. We could then save up for a place of our own.

The time arrived and I arranged for a registered child minder to care for my daughter and I worked for a secretarial agency until I could get a permanent job.

We couldn't save a lot of money but we tried hard and almost had enough for a deposit on a house. We had to borrow a small amount from my father-in-law and bought a house in Shaw near Oldham.

Juggling work and everything else was a work of art, we managed, but eventually the strain affected our marriage and sadly we split up. I then had to go cap in hand to my gran and ask could my daughter and I go and live with her. Once again my whole world had collapsed around me.

There was nothing for it I would have to start again. I couldn't give up my work as my parents would have to keep us both, which would have caused them great hardship. They did agree to look after my daughter whilst I worked.

No single parent benefits in those days! A few years later another relationship developed. I was given the deposit for a house, which my father had to stand guarantor for. All seemed to be going well when my partner was told he was being made redundant, as his family firm was being taken over by one of the big firms. He would receive the 'golden handshake' and would have to think what to do to earn a living as he was in

his mid- 40's and had never had
another job.

An opportunity came to buy a business
in Wales consisting of a guest house,
holiday flats, a caravan and enough left
to buy a boat to take angling trips. We
decided to go for it and moved there
just before Easter in 1973. I was a
complete novice but soon got to grips
with looking after guests, servicing the
flats for the next paying guests, and all
went well. Angling trips were booked
from the guest house and surplus trips
were given to an old guy who lived on a
boat in Bangor who didn't have a
telephone.

At Easter of the second year our
relationship began to fall apart, there
were issues between my partner and
my daughter which I won't go into.

I then realised I would have to do something. As my parents had brought my daughter up for the early part of her life I asked them to care for her permanently*. It was a very difficult time and I needed space to decide my future. I could not stay in this relationship so I asked the guy on the boat if I could stay there until I sorted my head out. He agreed I could for a trial period, so I packed a few possessions - my sea boots, my oil skins and my pressure cooker. I left a house full of stuff but that wasn't important, I was in a state of indecision, hurt, furious and very confused.

This was the start of a new way of life, albeit for a few days or maybe longer? I did eventually stay for 18 years, working as crew on a trawler. We lived aboard and worked hard from morning until night when out fishing, 16 hour days were the norm. I ended up with big muscles from pulling ropes, climbing a rope ladder several times a day when in port – no two days were the same there was always something to do even if it was only keeping warm. Several layers of clothing were essential during the winter. When the snow was on the mountains and the wind was blowing it was like a big freezer door being opened.

I learned a lot about life, boat terminology, net mending, gutting fish, mending engines and coping with emergencies, as the skipper used to say "money is no good out at sea, there's no hard shoulder, it's up to us to sort it out". The sea is one of the greatest things to sort the men out from the boys. You have to be real shipmates to spend 24/7 with each other living in a small cabin, and be self-sufficient. A generator provided the electricity, water was carried in a 5 gallon container, and you were always on duty even in port, when bad weather was around. In the bad winters when the ice formed you had to keep an area round the boat free or it would crush the wooden planks. Sometimes tree trunks or large pieces of timber came in with the tide. These had to be fended off, the tides have no mercy!

I soon found another philosophy on life - my priorities were different from the rat race I had been in. It was a huge learning curve, no fancy clothes, no make-up, everything had to be sensible. Whilst fishing your clothes got wet through hauling the catch aboard no food until the catch was gutted and put below, as that was our wage packet.

Then the disappointment when the fish went to market and the bottom had fallen out of the market for your fish. Sometimes it cost you more than you got back with the landing_charges cost of ice, diesel, nets, dock dues etc.

Our main payment was the way of life and happiness at doing something you enjoyed, despite the hardships. Money passed through your hands like quicksilver. We ate fish "8 days a week" during the fishing season and lived mainly on smoked fish during the winter. All money had to be earned between March and November. The fish are migratory and you would have had to travel many miles to earn a living. Winter time was spent getting the nets ready for the next season, overhauling the rigging, engine servicing, and keeping healthy. You had to be tough!

Sadly my husband the skipper, as he had become, passed away in 1993 he was 28 years older than me. I was devastated, I had nursed him for some years, not easy with basic facilities but we made light work of it. I had been so privileged to have had this way of life for that many years. People said it wouldn't last "a woman on a boat" but we proved them wrong, we were soul mates - so much in harmony.

I had nowhere to live but my parents invited me to stay with them. This again was difficult as I hadn't lived at home for over 30 years. Quite a culture shock! My father was 80yrs and my mother 77yrs, already set in their ways like myself.

The boat had to be sold which took some doing as the market wasn't good. I then had to get used to living ashore which was very difficult to adjust to. Back to the rat race! So much had changed since I last lived in society but I vowed I would not lose the values I had learned.

They also took my ship's cat in too who had never lived in a house. He was 16 years old and had only lived on fresh fish which was readily available but now had to be coaxed with tin food! What a come down!

We all got on well together but then tragedy struck again the same year when my father passed away. They had been married for 54 years. He had been caring for my mother who hadn't had good health for many years, so I stepped into the brink and became her carer.

Two widows in one house of different generations did have its ups and downs and comedy! Good job we both had a sense of humour and appreciated the irony.

My dilemma was how I could earn a living again on my own. It took two years before I could make a decision. I had no knowledge of computers, so office work was out of the question. I was aged 50 and having been self-employed for so long, and having a determined nature I didn't think I could take orders from anyone. I had also led an outdoor life so offices would be too claustrophobic.

Eventually I started my own business with a unit in Afflecks Palace selling second hand haberdashery, repairing clothes, recycling clothes, it was called The Button Queen. A year later I invested my boat money in a country and western shop which I called The Boot Scoot and Boogie Store. My stock was mostly authentic from the USA. In the 90's line dancing had taken off big style and there were no shops in Manchester so I had found a niche market. I was very successful until the big stores jumped on the band wagon and authentic clothes went out of fashion. In 1997 I met my present husband, and once again tied the knot! We ran a country and western club in Stretford. This also tied in with my business.

In 2001 the realised that I would have to close down as trade was very poor, and I didn't want to go bankrupt. So it was the end of an era. I was very sad but I had to cut my losses.

I have had a wonderful life, been so lucky, despite the hardships and sadness. I would still do the same things if I had my time again. One day I will write my story in full, it will be full of irony, comedy and serious stuff, but it will be a legacy for my grand-children, recording the exploits of their grandmother. If I don't do this nobody else can tell the tale - only me!

*My daughter and I are now reconciled, explanations given, and we are the best of friends. This stage took some years - after all there was a big gap in our relationship, hurtful on both sides. We now speak regularly on the phone as she has always lived many miles away. She married a man training for the ministry, who qualified to become a minister in the Methodist Church. They have four lovely girls and recently a great granddaughter.

October 2011

MUM'S POEMS

BIRDS IN WINTER

The trees are so bare
And cold is the air.
As the wind howls down from the
North
Huddled together
Against the bitter cold weather
The birds seek each other for warmth.

They wait and they wait
No sound do they make
For their breakfast
Since the breaking of dawn.
The window then raised
Crumbs scattered around.

Then down they all swoop to the
ground.

FAIRY FROLICS
(for Janet -Granddaughter)

In the grey light just at dawning,
As my eyes give up their sleep,
From my window, as I'm yawning
At the garden lawn I peep.

Fairy rings I see before me,
Glistening in the morning dew.
How I wish I'd been awake then
Just to see the things they do.

All the flowers still are sleeping,
Nodding in the summer breeze.
They must have seen the fairies dancing
Or slide along the bright moonbeams.

As I look I try to picture,
All their frolics through the night.

Fairies, pixies, elves, together
Dancing in the bright moonlight.

How the fairies sang, in greeting
As their Queen came floating down.
Her tiny gown all bright and shining
On a cloud of thistledown.

All that's left are toadstool houses
Where they rested through the night.
I'm so glad they chose my garden
For their dance this summer night.

GUESS WHO?

Hair cut short and darkish brown
With lads she plays around.
Hazel eyes and freckled nose,
No simpering grace, or girlish pose.

Skating, shooting, cricket too,
There's no end of things to do.
Marbles, bikes, and football games,
Dolls and prams are much too tame.

Swimming soon she will be able
No hide and seek beneath the table,
Running, rounders, climbing trees,
No fancy frocks, but trousers please.

School is not her favourite pastime,
Glad she is, when it's the last time,
Holidays for her could last forever,
She's no time for being clever.

Still she goes when she is able
Learning sums and 12 times table.
History, English, and art are funny
But she'd rather feed the bunny.

Moody, sulky too at times
Her laughter rings like tinkling chimes.
She has a most delightful grin
With two little dimples in her chin.

Her family of pets is ever growing,
Hamster, bird and puppy knowing
She loves them with all her heart
And from each one she ne'er will part.

Here's the story of dear Elaine
Let's read it all just once again,
And thank the Lord who sent her here
To help and light each day so drear.

GYPSY ROSALIE

I wish I was a gypsy,
Like Gypsy Rosalie.
With crystal ball and earrings,
The future I would see.

I'd stand outside my waggon,
All painted gay and light,
Inviting all to come there
To view their future bright.

They'd cross my hand with silver,
And drink my cups of tea,
So's I could read the tea leaves
And foretell their future bright.

I'd wander along the wayside,
Living a life so free.
Under the stars I'd sleep at night
Like Gypsy Rosalie.

HARVEST HYMN

Blackberries in the hedgerows
Are hanging ripe and good
And nuts for winter storage
Are growing in the wood.

Chorus:
How good and great our Father's care
To send the harvest everywhere.

Apples in the orchard
Are juicy big and sweet,
Mushrooms in the meadow
Spring up around our feet.

Chorus:
How good and great our Father's care
To send the harvest everywhere.

Potatoes in the garden

Are picked and stored away
And farmers in the fields
Are busy making hay.

Chorus:
How good and great our Father's care
To send the harvest everywhere.

THE CHRISTMAS TREE

The Christmas tree is wondrous fair,
Laden with gifts for us to share.
The lights, they gleam and shine so
bright.
Hurrah! Hurrah! For Christmas night.

The table is full of things to eat,
There's jelly and turkey and some sort
of meat.
The family all sit round in paper hats,
Whilst aunties and uncles enjoy cosy
chats.

The balloons are blown up full and
round,
Whilst baby sleeps on without a sound
Amongst the noise and laughter jolly.
Hurrah! For mistletoe and holly!

Santa comes in with gown a- bustle.

The gifts unwrapped with paper a-
rustle.
A book for Bill, a doll for Jane,
Johnnie shouts, "Gosh a train!"
The day is over, the lights are low.
The visitor's dressed and homeward go.
The children climb upstairs to bed
Whilst the Christmas star shines
overhead.

<u>WHY?</u>

Why is the world supposed to be round
When it looks so flat to me?
Why does the moon stay up in the sky
When it might fall down on me?

Why do my eyes see all they see
Yet, when they're shut I still see?
Why do I shed sweet tears of joy
When I'm supposed to be happy, beats
me?

Why do people hate and be nasty
When there's so much love around?
Why should the baddies get off free
While the goodies fall down to the
ground?

Why? Oh Why? Pie in the sky

Beats me!

THE END

ABOUT THE AUTHOR

Sylvia was born during World War II in North Manchester, now lives in Ordsall, Salford.

Worked as a secretary, ran a café and guest house, crewed as a deck hand on a trawler, came ashore and became a self - employed trader in haberdashery then country and western clothing.

Joined a local writing group and wrote her first poem in 2010 as well as anecdotes, articles and fiction.